HART PICTURE ARCHIVES

Oriental Designs

Compiled by Robert Sietsema

Hart Publishing Company, Inc. ● New York City

COPYRIGHT © 1978 HART PUBLISHING COMPANY, INC.
NEW YORK, NEW YORK 10012

ISBN NO. 08055-1267-5 (PAPERBACK 08055-0330-7)

MANUFACTURED IN THE UNITED STATES OF AMERICA

CONTENTS

HOW TO USE THIS BOOK

ORIENTAL DESIGNS is a collection of over 250 pictures of many periods, culled from 17 known sources. These pictures have been subdivided into 4 categories.

All these pictures are in the public domain. They derive from magazines, books, and pictures copyrighted by Hart Publishing Company, now released to the public for general use.

So as not to clutter a caption, the source is given an abbreviated designation. Full publication data may be found in the *Sources* section, in which all sources are listed in alphabetical order, with the full title of the book or magazine, the publisher, and the date of publication. The *Sources* section commences on page 79.

Three of the pictures are halftones, and they are designated by a square symbol □ at the end of the caption. These pictures, too, are suitable for reproduction, but the user is alerted to rescreen such a picture or convert it into line. All other pictures can be reproduced directly in line.

Chinese Designs

Plum blossom and magpie, embroidery design. *Folk Designs*

Carp leaping the Dragon Gate to become dragons, embroidery design. *Folk Designs*

Papercut Design

Chinese Designs continued

Porcelain vase decoration, 2 sides. *L'Art, Vol. 24*

Ancient porcelain plate. *L'Art, Vol. 33*

Chinese Designs continued

Squirrel and grapes. *Papercut Design*

Papercut Design

Ancient tapestry. *L'Art, Vol. 37*

Papercut Design

Ancient tapestry. *L'Art, Vol. 37*

Rabbit *Papercut Design*

Papercut Design

Papercut Design

Chinese Designs continued

French plate, 18th century. *L'Art, Vol. 23*

Dragon and tiger fighting, embroidery design. *Folk Designs*

Papercut Design

Papercut Design

Chinese Designs continued

Procelain design by Kien-Long, dated 1888. *L'Art, Vol. 28*

Chinese Designs continued

Woodcut. *Bamboo Studio*

Various folk motifs. *Folk Designs*

Unicorn, embroidery design. *Folk Designs*

Chinese Designs continued

Hart Publishing

Goldfish. *Folk Designs*

Chrysanthemum. *Papercut Design*

Ho Sian-Gu, the patron saint of housewives, with a lotus flower. *Chinesische Teppich*

Dschang Guo, the patron saint of doctors. seated on a white ass. *Chinesische Teppich*

Moonlit landscape. *Folk Designs*

Chinese Designs continued

Diaper Ornament. *Outlines*

Diaper Ornament. *Outlines*

Chinese Designs continued

Fabric design. *Chinesische Teppich*

臨流
十竹齋寫

Woodcut. *Bamboo Studio*

Chinese Designs continued

Laquered box designs, 19th century. *L'Art, Vol. 16*

Serpent and flower, embroidery design. *Folk Designs*

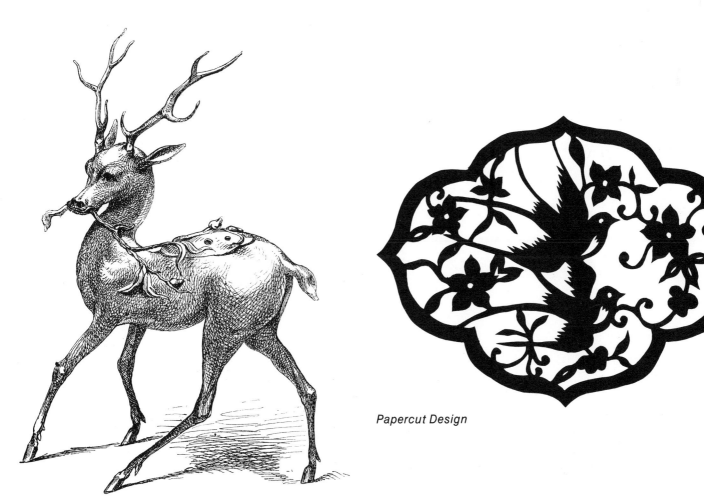

Ancient bronze symbolical statuette. *L'Art, Vol. 17*

Papercut Design

Indian Designs

Painted tissue, 17th century. *L'Art, Vol. 22*

Foliage from cotton printer's blocks, 19th century. *Pattern Design*

Fabric design. *La toile*

Indian Designs continued

Two designs made from the same cotton printer's block. *Pattern Design*

Enlargement of the block used for designs above.

Fabric design. *La toile*

Indian Designs continued

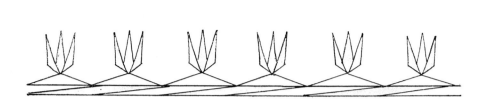

Manuscript ornament. *L'Art*

Sixteenth century tapestry. *L'Art, Vol. 32*

Cotton print pattern. *Pattern Design*

Cotton print pattern. *Pattern Design*

Indian Designs continued

Cotton print pattern. *Pattern Design*

Manuscript ornament, 17th century. *L'Art, Vol. 34*

Linen curtain, 18th century. *La toile* □

Indian Designs continued

Cotton print pattern. *Pattern Design*

Cotton print pattern. *Pattern Design*

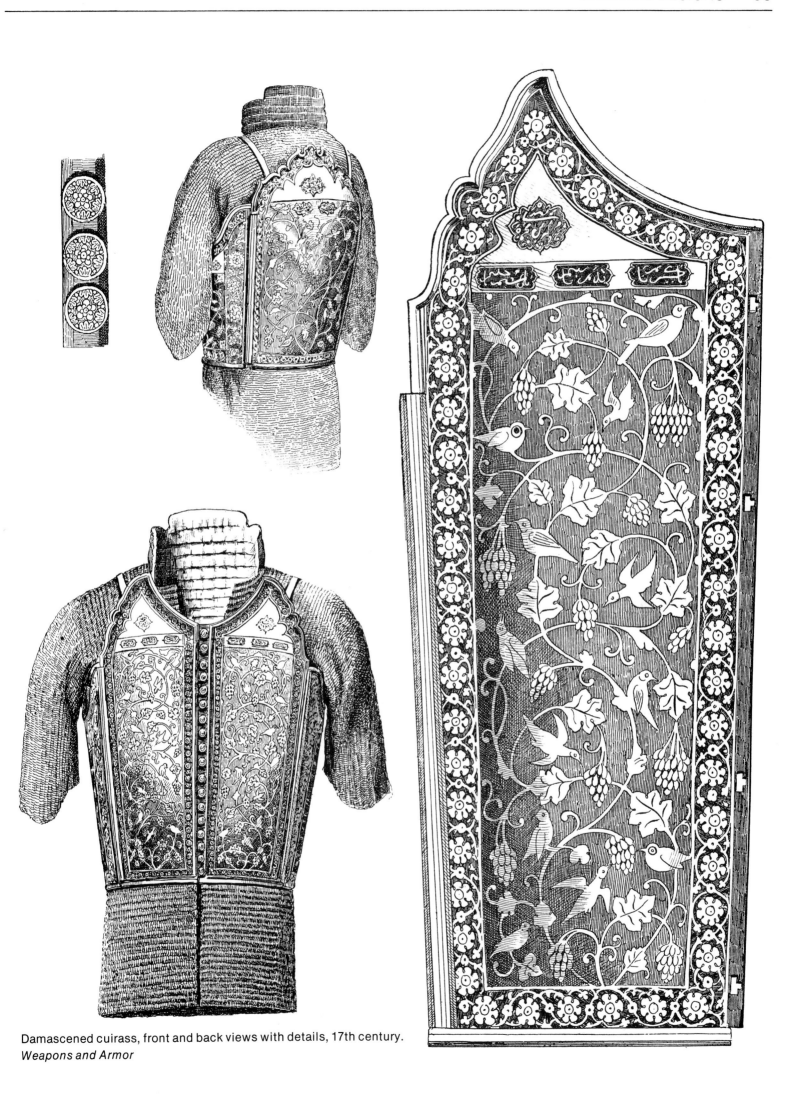

Damascened cuirass, front and back views with details, 17th century.
Weapons and Armor

Indian Designs continued

Cotton print pattern. *Pattern Design*

Cotton print pattern. *Pattern Design*

Painted tissue, 17th century. *L'Art, Vol. 22*

Japanese Designs

Japanese Stencil Designs

Variations on motifs taken from ancient family crests. *Design Motifs*

Dry brush drawing. *Artistic Japan*

Japanese Designs continued

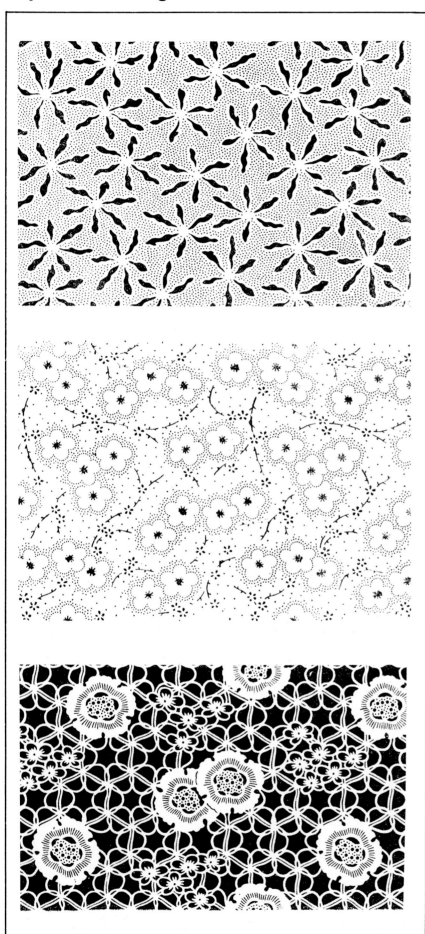

Tissue designs. *L'Art, Vol. 19*

Philosopher on the back of a flying stork, bronze hanging ornament. *L'Art, Vol. 13*

Sword guard, 18th century. *L'Art, Vol. 32*

Fish folk motif, in bronze. *L'Art, Vol. 31*

Japanese Stencil Designs

Japanese Stencil Designs

Tissues with star motifs. *L'Art, Vol. 28*

Ancient tapestry design. *L'Art, Vol. 37*

Bird folk motif, in bronze. *L'Art, Vol. 14*

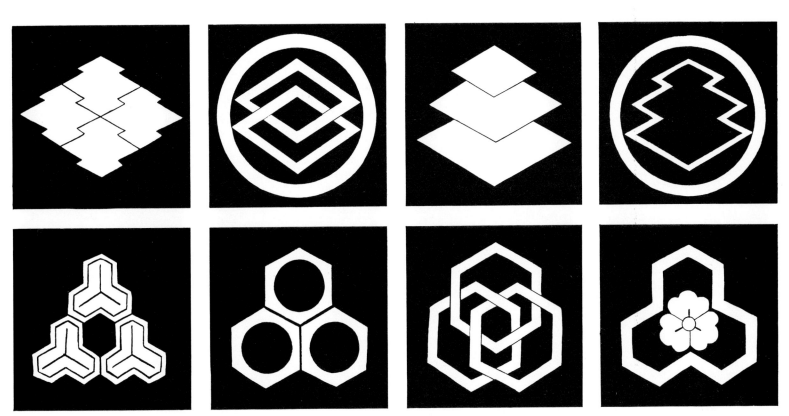

Motifs from family crests. *Design Motifs*

Japanese Stencil Designs

Japanese Designs continued

Nineteenth century fabric design. *L'Art, Vol. 34*

Dry brush drawing. *Artistic Japan*

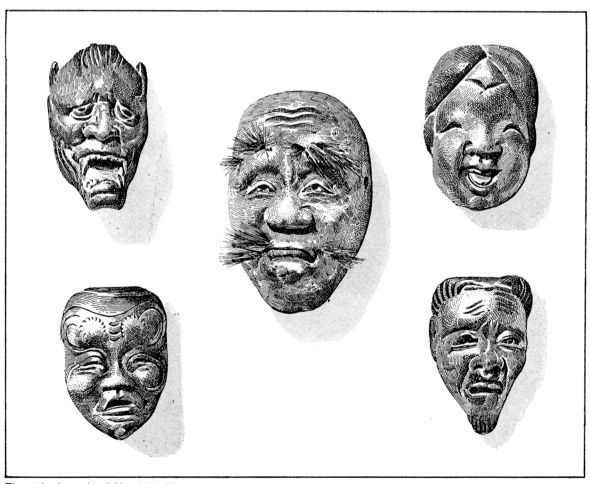

Theatrical masks. *L'Art, Vol. 32*

Powdered ornament. *Outlines*

Powdered ornament. *Outlines*

Tissue design. *L'Art, Vol. 29*

Japanese Designs continued

Variations on two motifs taken from ancient family crests; *top*, flower diamond motifs; *bottom*, gingko leaf motifs.   *Design Motifs*

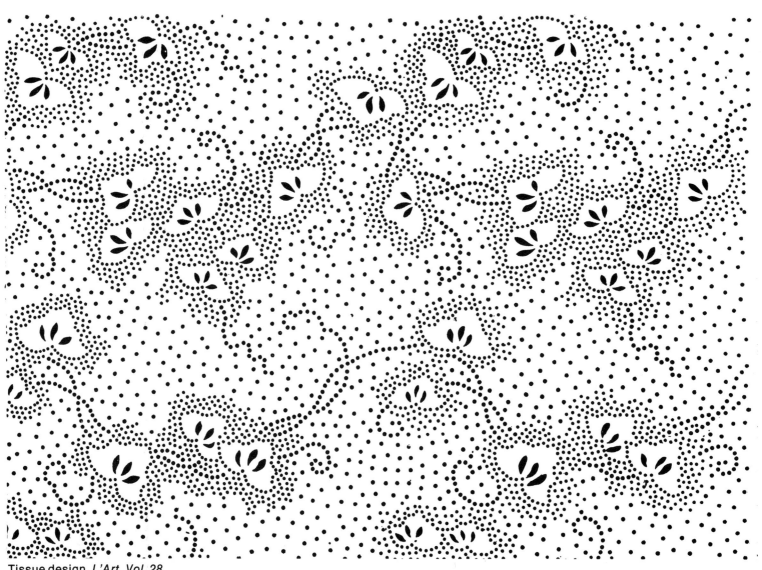

Water color by celebrated artist Hokou Sai. *L'Art, Vol. 27* □

Japanese Designs continued

Ink drawing. *Hachi-jo*

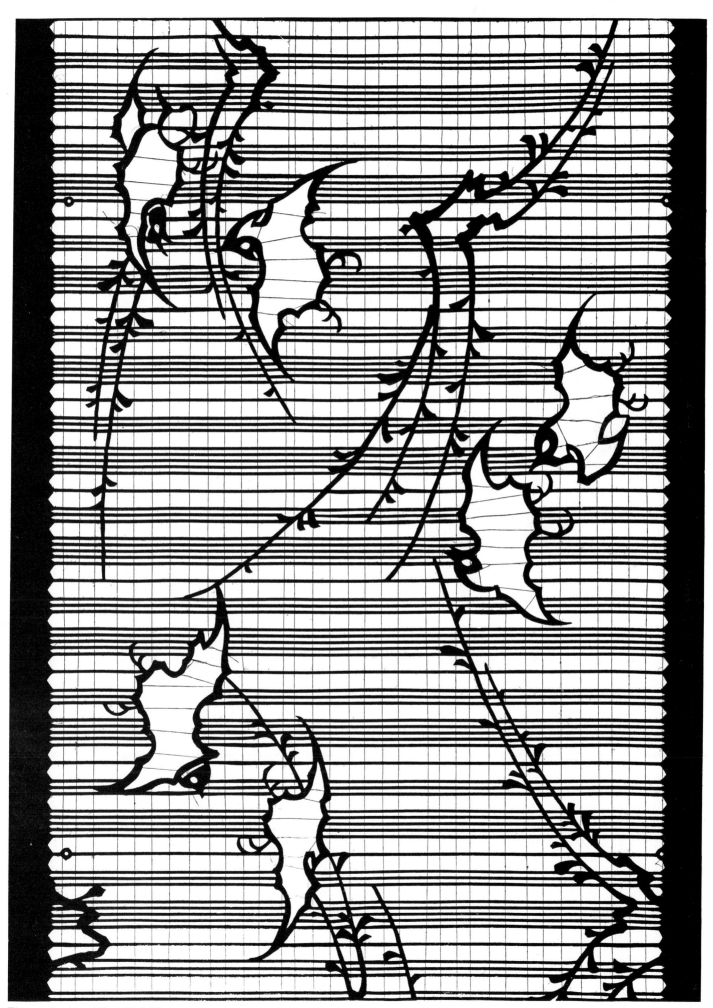

Tissue design. *L'Art, Vol. 26*

Japanese Designs continued

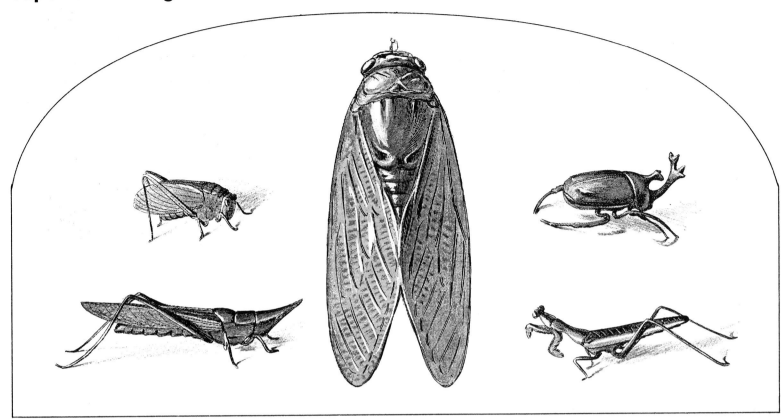

Insect folk motifs, in bronze. *L'Art, Vol. 31*

Tissue design. *L'Art, Vol. 29*

Powdered ornament. *Outlines*

Two hand-painted plates, early 20th century. *L'Art, Vol. 31*

Japanese Designs continued

Foliage motifs. *Outlines*

Fabric design. *L'Art, Vol. 33* □

Tissue design. *L'Art, Vol. 29*

Japanese Designs continued

Japanese Stencil Designs

Japanese Stencil Designs

Tissue design. *L'Art, Vol. 29*

Seventeenth century sword guards. *L'Art*

Persian Designs

Diaper ornament. *Outlines*

Hand-painted plate, 18th century. *L'Art, Vol. 32*

Persian Designs continued

Carpet design, 16th century. *Industrial Arts*

Hand-painted plate, 17th century. *L'Art, Vol. 36*

Persian Designs continued

Ancient jade screen with gems set in gold. *L'Art, Vol. 9*

Drawing by Mirza Akbar, early 19th century. *Pattern Design*

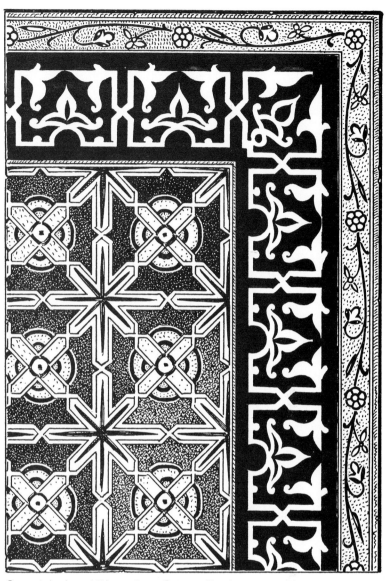

Carpet design, 14th century. *Pattern Design*

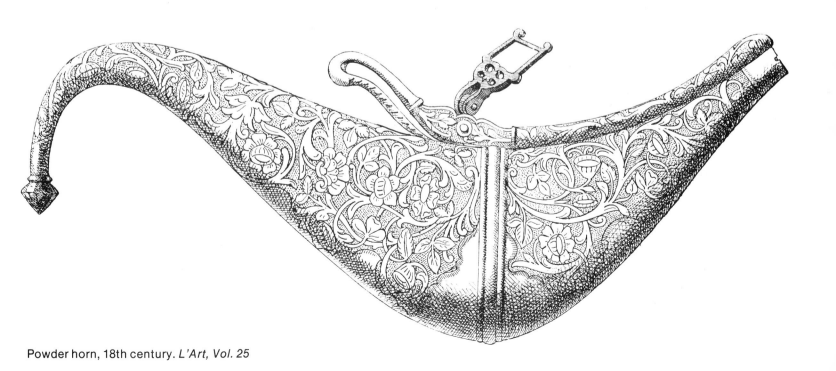

Powder horn, 18th century. *L'Art, Vol. 25*

Persian Designs continued

Illuminated manuscript page, 17th century. *L'Art, Vol. 30*

Illuminated manuscript page, 17th century. *L'Art, Vol. 30*

Persian Designs continued

Carpet Design, 14th century. *Pattern Design*

Islamic silk design, 14th century. *Pattern Design*

Woven silk fabric, 17th century. *Pattern Design*

Conventional foliage. *Pattern Design*

Persian Designs continued

Book cover design, 17th century. *L'Art, Vol. 28* □

Ceramic ornament, 18th century. *L'Art, Vol. 27*

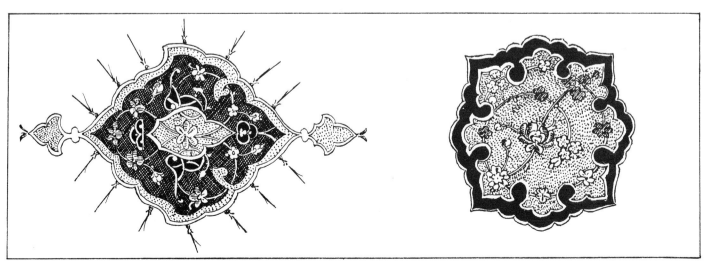

Arabic manuscript ornament. *L'Art, Vol. 18*

Persian Designs continued

Drawing by Mirza Akbar, early 19th century. *Pattern Design*

Palmette pattern on enameled bricks, 6th century b.c. *Pattern Design*

Ceramic ornament, 18th century. *L'Art, Vol. 27*

Persian Designs continued

end view

Axe heads ornamented with gold, 18th century. *Weapons and Armor*

Detail of a 16th century carpet, in silk. *Hart Publishing*

Wall tile designs, 16th century. *Pattern Design*

Motifs from a Persian carpet found in perpetual ice in the Soviet Union, over 2400 years old. *Hart Publishing*

Persian Designs continued

Sixteenth century plate. *L'Art, Vol. 41*

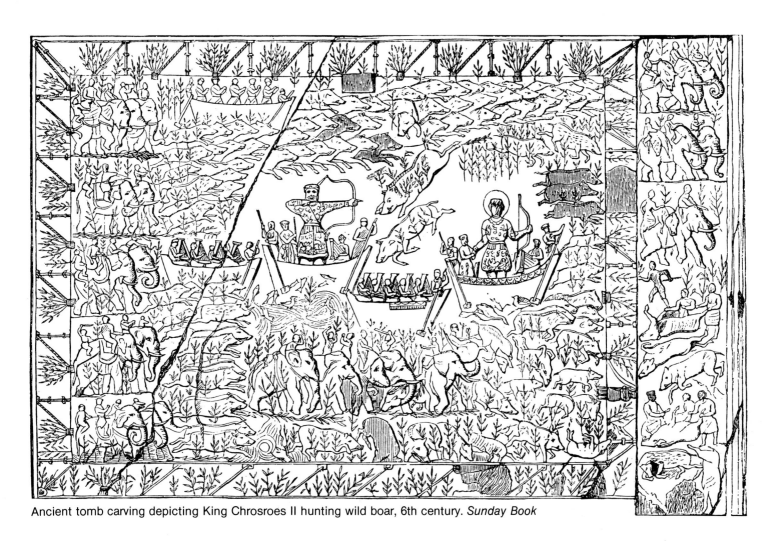

Ancient tomb carving depicting King Chrosroes II hunting wild boar, 6th century. *Sunday Book*

Book ornament. *L'Art, Vol. 22*

Assorted arabesques. *L'Art*

Persian Designs continued

Designs on various gun barrels, 19th century. *L'Art, Vol. 47*

Hand-painted plates, 16th century. *L'Art, Vol. 41*

Persian Designs continued

Arabic manuscript page. *Hart Publishing*

L'Art, Vol. 16

Arabesques. *L'Art, Vol. 27*

Ornamental shield. *L'Art, Vol. 12*

Miniature painting. *Harper's*

Arabesques. *L'Art, Vol. 17*

Manuscript ornaments.
L'Art, Vol. 8

Embroidered cloth. *Harper's*

SOURCES

ARTISTIC JAPAN; full title, *Artistic Japan, a Monthly Illustrated Journal of the Arts and Industries.* S. Low: London, 1888-1891.

BAMBOO STUDIO (four vols.). Fun Cheng Yeu. Peking: World Book Co., 1952.

CHINESISCHE TEPPICH, DER. Hackmack, Adolf. Hamburg: Fredrichsen, circa 1920.

DESIGN MOTIFS. Mizoguchi, Saburo. Tokyo: Shibundo, 1973.

FOLK DESIGNS; full title, *Chinese Folk Designs.* Hawley, W.M. New York: Dover Publications, 1971.

HARPER'S; full title, *Harper's New Monthly Magazine.* New York: Harper & Brothers, 1851-1888.

HACHI-JO; full title, *History of the Isle of Hachi-jo.* Hobusai. Tokyo, 1816.

HART PUBLISHING. Illustrations by artists at Hart Publishing Company, Inc., New York

INDUSTRIAL ARTS; full title, *Chefs-D'Oeuvre of the Industrial Arts.* Burty, Phillipe. New York: D. Appleton & Co., 1869.

JAPANESE STENCIL DESIGNS. Tuer, Andrew W. New York: Dover Publications, 1967.

L'ART; full title, *L'Art Pour Tous, Encyclopedie de l'Art Industriel et Decoratif.* Reiber, Emile, ed. Paris: A. Morel et C., 1861-1906.

LA TOILE. Paris, circa 1900.

OUTLINES; full title, *Outlines of Ornament in the Leading Styles.* Audsley, W. & G. New York: Scribner, 1882.

PAPERCUT DESIGN. Available from China Books and Periodicals. 125 Fifth Avenue, New York City.

PATTERN DESIGN; original title, *Traditional Methods of Pattern Designing.* Christie, Archibald H. New York: Dover Publications, 1967 (original publication date, 1910).

SUNDAY BOOK; full title, *The Pictorial Sunday Book.* Kitto, John, ed. London: The London Printing and Publishing Company, Ltd., no date.

WEAPONS & ARMOR. Sietsema, Robert. New York: Hart Publishing Company, 1978.

HART PICTURE ARCHIVES

AMERICAN DESIGNS

THE ANIMAL KINGDOM

BORDERS & FRAMES

CHAIRS

COMPENDIUM

DESIGNS OF THE ANCIENT WORLD

DINING & DRINKING

EUROPEAN DESIGNS

GOODS & MERCHANDISE

HOLIDAYS

HUMOR, WIT, & FANTASY

JEWELRY

ORIENTAL DESIGNS

TRADES & PROFESSIONS

WEAPONS & ARMOR

WEATHER

TITLES IN PREPARATION

FACES

JARS, BOWLS, & VASES

TYPOGRAPHICAL ORNAMENTS